the

Extraordinary

Ordinary

A BOOK OF HOURS

HOSPICE and PALLIATIVE CARE of GREENSBORO

Hospice • Beacon Place • Kids Path • Counseling and Education Center

The Extraordinary Ordinary
A Book of Hours

Text by Cynthia Adams
Design by 29 & Company

www.hospicegso.org

First Printing April 2005
ISBN 0-9700015-1-7
Printed in the United States of America

DEAR READER, Hospice and Palliative Care of Greensboro commissioned this anniversary book in order to share the remarkable, transformative beauty of our daily experiences. This intimate book contains images and impressions lifted from any given day of any given week. We do this in honor of 25 years of ordinary folks doing extraordinary things in our community from Monday sunrise through to Sunday vespers.

These glimpses into our work demonstrate movingly why Hospice is considered one of the "great, quiet revolutions of our time."

Our history is steeped in the tradition of grass-roots volunteerism; Henry Nowen,

Messenger by Gary Lee Price

author and priest, might have characterized these early pioneers, as well as those involved in the movement today, as the beloved…In his 1992 book, *Life of the Beloved,* he explains that "becoming the beloved is pulling the truth…from above, down to the ordinariness of what I am…doing from hour to hour." He precisely describes the beloved who grace our lives through Hospice and are represented by the ordinary stories writer Cynthia Adams has so beautifully captured.

THOUSANDS OF SUPPORTERS, caregivers,

corporate leaders, individual angels, and unseen hands have guided us along our way. Twenty-five years ago, Hospice began in Greensboro. A first board of enthusiastic hard-working volunteers was formed after the Hospice movement reached Greensboro in the late 1970s and the first official meeting of the membership of interested citizens was held in 1980. The organization was born. Two part-time staff (a nurse and social worker) along with a handful of volunteers, found their way to the donated basement office of the Public Health Department, were trained, and set to work.

Dr. John Lusk made the first Hospice referral in 1982. Hospice offered loving and compassionate support that allowed those with terminal illnesses to be cared for in the comfort of home. Moses Cone Hospital responded to the Hospice program, with volunteers and vision, offering a joint venture in 1984 which is recognized to this day as model hospice-hospital collaboration.

Naming names, work, ideas, or reasons this succeeded is dangerous business, yet some names simply must be said…while others, equally essential cannot. All these names are written in our collective soul. I was welcomed to this community in 1985 by hospice pioneers including Eloise Lewis, Bill Trent, Stewart Rogers and Gene Tranbarger, to name only a few. For over two decades I have been inspired and blessed by working alongside professional colleagues, as well as tireless volunteers. For their exceptional gifts and commitment over time, I note folks like Lou Wallace, Marion Taylor, Carole Bruce, Tim Rice, Charlotte Chatlain, Alice Cooke and Eleanor Lindley. So many others work earnestly and zealously still, with the same earnestness of our founders; you will read their stories.

The grace notes within this book also offer answers to the question we are asked again and again: "What can *I* do?" "How can *I* serve?"

The Junior League toiled to support our first bereavement education initiatives in the public schools. Joe and Jeff Bostic spearheaded a celebrity golf tournament for a decade. The First Presbyterian Church provided us with a lovely early home and then Cone Mills donated property for a permanent campus setting. The leadership gift to build the Hospice Center, which also included the Counseling and Education Center, came from the Nussbaum family, honoring their parents, Vic and Terry Nussbaum. Joseph M. Bryan, Jr. and Bill and Clarence Jones took the lead, respectively, to expand our facilities to include Beacon Place and Kids Path on the hospice campus. Every community foundation, the United Way, and individual donors offering $5 and $10 memorial tributes, have also faithfully supported our mission for the past quarter century.

HOSPICE'S STORY is historical, broad, and yet achingly personal. This is illustrated every day of every week of every single year.

We see what is possible, what can manifest in ordinary people — the ideas, the noble strength, the everyday sweat and sometimes tears — that makes the extraordinary happen. It has happened for these past 25 years, and it will happen again tomorrow.

We who have been touched by Hospice — each family, volunteer, staff member, and partner in this magnificent adventure — are profoundly

grateful for the privilege of experiencing the extraordinary. We thank you, one and all, for making this possible.

Pam Barrett

— *Pam Barrett,* PRESIDENT AND CEO

Grieving people need to freely express feelings, including anger and tears. Do not feel you need to change the subject if someone begins to express pain. The sharing of pain helps dissipate it.

BELLA RISES EARLY, and chooses a toy before rousing the household. Even at dawn she radiates goodwill. She is aptly named; Bella is "beautiful" in Italian.

She paces excitedly as her friend Becky makes coffee and dresses. Mondays are Bella's favorite day; she misses Hospice during weekends. Soon Becky and Bella head off to their Hospice jobs, where Becky is a counselor and Bella has a full schedule assisting Becky as a pet therapist.

Bella's empathy grew out of her personal losses. She was abandoned then adopted by Becky's sister, Libby. Life smoothed out until Bella lost her beloved companion Huck. Bella grieved for Huck, growing listless and unresponsive. Becky began taking Bella along to work to console her.

Bella rapidly became a welcomed part of Hospice life, greeting staff and visitors. She began accompanying Becky on occasional counseling sessions with bereaved children. Bella was highly intuitive, seeming to know exactly who needed her. When a child buried their face into Bella's fur and confessed their pain, Bella silently empathized.

She now works with about 10 children on any given week. As they walk, or play fetch, she sometimes senses a heaviness release from the child. With her, children relearn gentle calm, and playful joy.

Bella's tail wags happily at the very thought of her good work, for it is the better part of this dog's life.

— *Bella*, PET THERAPY

"The conquest of the fear of death is the recovery of life's joy."
— Joseph Campbell

URSULA'S BROWN EYES LIGHT whenever she smiles, and she smiles often. Yet Ursula's face clouds recalling the day her world exploded. She returned home from school, shocked to discover a funeral wreath on the door and a house filled with strangers. Her beloved grandfather was dead. But in those days, young children were shielded from death and especially from funerals.

"I am an advocate for letting the child decide about the funeral," Ursula says firmly.

The years flew by. When she turned 16, Ursula's grandmother and three friends struck a deal. They bought her a "sky-blue, Carolina blue, 1978 Chevette." In exchange, Ursula drove them to funerals, weddings, and hair appointments. The widows pelted her with wit, wisdom, and laughter. Ursula absorbed it all.

At the wheel of a blue Chevette Ursula learned that as surely as people could have joyful lives, "they can also have a good death." Now the words of the knowing widows drive her philosophies.

Now a Hospice administrator, Ursula is driven "to change the culture of how people die."

— *Ursula,* CLINICAL ADMINISTRATION

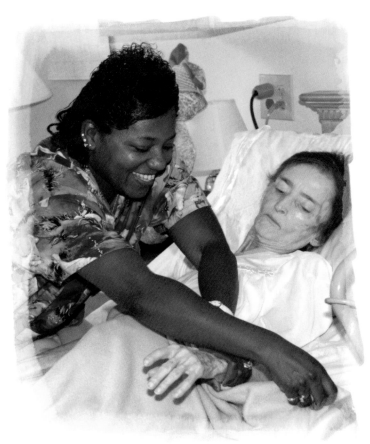

It is normal when grieving to feel exhausted. Housework and errands may seem overwhelming. Allow yourself time to resume routine duties, and become more attentive to your own needs.

SHARON CRACKLES WITH ENERGY even

though she has bathed five patients today. She smoothes her tidily braided hair, explaining how she honors the dignity of her patients.

She makes certain each patient has a smile on their face before she leaves them, no matter how great their worries. Worries are something she understands.

Sharon has known grinding despair. She cried every single morning for eight years on her former job. "'Little Bit,' you ain't going nowhere… You're here to stay," fellow mill workers chided her.

But Sharon was going somewhere. She enrolled in nurses' training and began the tender work that is "her fantasy."

"I feel like I'm very important here. I do nothing that no one else does, but *I feel special.*"

Sharon makes it her work to discover what might make the patient less care-worn. Before she leaves, there's time for a tender hug, a squeezed hand, or a moment to soothe the frazzled caregiver. She once returned to straighten a patient's home after her work day ended, because the disarray haunted her.

And then, only then, "Little Bit" goes home, where her own family waits.

— *Sharon,* NURSE TECH

"In the landscape of Death we feel more like foreigners. We don't know what to expect;
we don't speak the language; we can't read the thoughts of God.
And yet all roads on the spiritual journey lead here, to death, the soul, and God."

– Elizabeth Lesser

GOOD GRIEF.

"There *is* such a thing as good grief!" declares Lou, who will meet a bereavement group this evening. "My work is all about hope and healing. I see the Phoenix rising *over and over and over* again."

"People have to have permission to do the grief work…But everybody tries to talk you out of it," Lou explains. Society urges those grieving to rush through a process that cannot be rushed.

"People need to learn that losing someone we love isn't about getting over it — it's about living with it."

Lou points out the Hospice atrium where she has married former bereavement clients. She talks about celebrations held in the very place where broken hearts first began mending.

"I get to serve people as they move into new meaning, constructing new lives. The happy stories are such good stories, too. People say, 'I admire you for doing that work. It must be depressing.' It's *not!* It's affirming, loving care."

— *Lou*, CHAPLAINCY AND
BEREAVEMENT COUNSELING

Don't worry that you may not know what to say when comforting a grieving friend. Your quiet and supportive presence is valuable. "Saying nothing sometimes says the most," observed Emily Dickinson.

IT IS CRISP AND COOL at Wiley Elementary school. In the auditorium, a volunteer troupe prepares the *Aarvy Aardvark Finds Hope* puppet show. The show began through Hospice's *Living with Loss* program. For 15 years it has moved through Greensboro schools, due to the Junior League's initial funding and scores of unseen hands behind the curtain.

Some of the puppeteers once knew Julie, a child with a brain tumor. After Julie's death, friends and neighbors trooped the show for years to area schools. Many who troupe Aarvy Aardvaark do so to honor a lost child.

Today, 30 third graders watch the antics of Aarvy and his forest friends. The puppets tell a story of loss and renewal. The children's hands shoot up afterwards when asked what grief and loss are. They have lost many things: money, security, and lives. One child's father is in prison. Another child's father just lost his job. One boy says sadly his twin cousins died, "because they didn't get enough air."

But only 10 of the 30 children raise a tentative hand when the teacher asks, "Do you have someone you can talk to?"

— *Aarvy*, KIDS PATH PUPPET

"Let yourself be silently drawn,
  by the stronger pull of what you really love."

— *Rumi*

IT'S A GOOD TIME TO KNIT, Shannon decides.

Heck, she thinks, it's always a good time to knit.

Shannon is among 88 members of The Busy Bee Crafters, volunteers knitting items for Hospice patients and Women's Hospital newborns.

She giggles, confessing, "The Busy Bee Crafters was not the first name I picked…our first name was The Happy Hookers." She ruefully admits they were able to better recruit with their tamer name. Shannon alone produces nearly 50 afghans and baby blankets yearly. (A fellow Busy Bee, Corinne, once trumped Shannon by producing twice as much.)

Open her closet, Shannon confesses, and you'll find — yarn. She also teaches knitting to anyone who wants to learn at a local Recreation Center.

"I love it! I live, breathe, and drink it," she declares without dropping a stitch.

— *Shannon,* BUSY BEE CRAFTERS

In any major city, at least a fourth of the working residents cope with bereavement, threat of unemployment, or illness.

THE TODDLER'S FEET pump joyfully as Kate, a social worker, joins her on a quilt. Anslyn wears bubble gum pink shorts, and clutches a rag doll. Kate produces a teaching doll dubbed "Trina Two Tubes," and a miniature doctor's kit. Anslyn wiggles happily as Kate demonstrates with a doll-sized stethoscope and aspirator.

Kate grins. "Would you like to help me clear the doll's trachea?"

Anslyn's tiny hands flex; she coos happily and reaches for the doll. A Kids Path nurse's husband modified "Trina" with a tiny tracheotomy and feeding tube for teaching and therapeutic child's play.

After "clearing" the doll's trachea, Anslyn pulls up the doll's shirt, exposing Trina's feeding tube. An oximeter is clipped to the toddler's gyrating toe. The meter glows as she playfully pushes her heel against Kate. Inches away, a ventilator pumps steadily. Anslyn has hypotonia, but is so improved she can disconnect herself from the ventilator. When she does it emits a warning "beep," but Anslyn successfully tolerates nearly 25 minutes off the ventilator — a very good sign.

Kate packs "Trina" away to leave as the child watches closely. As Kate disappears from the nursery with Anslyn's mother, a beep sounds. The mother laughs; Anslyn wants them to stay, she explains.

"She's figured it all out," Kate agrees. "She's so smart." When the women return to the nursery, Anslyn's eyes alight and she grins triumphantly.

— *Anslyn*, 2, KIDS PATH PATIENT

"First, keep the peace within yourself, then you can bring peace to others."

– *Thomas a Kempis*

JOHN ONLY GOES WHERE INVITED, yet can never know what his reception will be. When he enters a patient's home, John knows full well he arrives as an icon: the "God person."

As the "God person" — or chaplain — John symbolizes all the good or bad God represents to that patient. He shrugs, explaining how it is natural that we each have defenses wrapped up in beliefs. Yet, in his mind, John is not an icon, but arrives simply as the Comforter.

John's first duty is listening to discover "who and where that person is." There is no formula, and no certain outcome. As Comforter, he walks alongside the patient in a journey from raw grief towards what he hopes will be resolution.

Illness can move us beyond damaged relationships, unmet goals, crisis and turmoil. Illness, John observes, can *heal*. John remains fascinated and buoyed by seeing good come of bad. This deeply comforts the Comforter.

"Even though a healing of the body is not possible, healing of the soul is."

— *John,* CHAPLAINCY AND
BEREAVEMENT COUNSELING

Grief is not something that needs remedied or "fixed." Nor is there
a timetable for grieving. Grief simply takes as long as it takes.

EDMUND AND ANTHNETTE were inseparable, but Wednesdays were special. On Wednesdays, Edmund always brought Anthnette a red rose when he picked her up at work — for 16 years. "He was an easy person to love," she says softly.

Anthnette's red curls tremble slightly when speaking about her husband, who died in a tragic workplace accident last year. Anthnette quietly retells how she has coped.

"Before Hospice, I couldn't have told my story."

Following Edmund's death, Anthnette felt she was "going crazy" with grief. At her sister's urging she turned to Hospice for counseling, later joining a bereavement group. On the first night, the group discussed personal experiences.

"We talked, cried, and we understood."

Anthnette met Brenda, who had lost her husband to cancer. The two women felt an instant bond. Following the meeting they exchanged phone numbers and began sharing dinners, coffees, and comfort.

"I said, 'Lord, I can make it,'" Anthnette smiles.

Anthnette indicates a handsome portrait of her husband taken days before the accident, pauses, and swallows hard.

"I'll be missing Edmund all my life, but I'm going to make it. At Hospice, that's where I get my strength."

— *Anthnette,* BEREAVEMENT SERVICES CLIENT

"Death is just a moment when dying ends."
    – Michael de Montaigne

CHERYL, A NURSE, and Jim, a volunteer, chat in the family room of the Hospice unit at Moses Cone Hospital. Two men in rumpled workmen's clothing appear, plopping wearily onto chairs. Jim gently greets them, offering fresh coffee. The men's slumped bodies convey exhaustion from keeping vigil with their dying mother.

Waiting is what they must do now; waiting is the hardest work they have ever known.

Cheryl pours herself a coffee, and leans against the doorway.

"I had a volunteer, Jennie, who taught me something," Cheryl says. "Jennie said that dying people teach you how to live. She was right."

Two teenage trainees, Stacey and Octavia, sidle up to Cheryl. They plan to one day become nurse assistants. One has youthful braids. The other wears vivid pink lipstick. Cheryl smiles knowingly at their unlined faces. They know only a little of life, her smile says. Here, they will learn more.

"When people come through that door," Cheryl says, indicating the Hospice unit's entry, "they're in a crisis." She sometimes bakes bread for patients and families in the unit's kitchen, explaining how homey smells are normal and comforting.

The trainees keep an awkward but respectful silence; bread baking isn't in their nursing textbooks. The men rise heavily from their chairs, smiling wanly and gratefully at Cheryl and Jim. They return to their mother's room. And wait.

— *The Hospice Unit,* MOSES CONE HOSPITAL

At least 22 million American households comprise the "Sandwich Generation,"
actively working while also caring for an aging or ill family member.
Research indicates women shoulder the burden of care.

A PEACEFUL PHOTOGRAPH of a lakeside cabin hangs behind Celia's desk. A jar holds rocks pulled from the shores of the Hudson River and Scotland's coast. Each are totems reminding Celia of moments plucked from the broad stream of life. Celia is happiest close to the earth, rooting out treasures that look like stones to others.

Celia served on the original Hospice board. A college professor had once encouraged his students to choose life-affirming work, Celia recalls. She met his challenge. "*This* is life affirming work. It's part of a community that never dies."

Now Celia's desk is piled high with folders filled with patient records, a departure from 30 years working in the field with the chronic and severely ill. Within the folders lie the layers of a life; each paper yields another insight into a person, not a condition. Celia humanizes the paper work by telling social workers and chaplains she supervises, "Hearing your stories gives me life, and breadth."

On weekends, Celia determinedly tends her garden. "When I plant the seeds, my husband jokes, 'Oh, dear God, help them to live. She needs for them not to die!'"

And Celia, swearing she's a bad gardener, smiles.

— *Celia*, CLINICAL SERVICES

"When the body sinks into death, the essence of man is revealed. Man is a knot,
a web, a mesh into which relationships are tied. Only those relationships matter...
I have never known for a man to think of himself when dying. Never."

— Antoine de Saint-Exupery

PEOPLE STIR IN THE HALLWAYS of Beacon

Place, a residential program on the Hospice campus, and coffee smells waft along. A patient watches a news program in the lounge as a volunteer delivers colorful hand-knitted shawls.

Pat runs the homey, deliberately non-institutional, program. She favors casual clothing over nurses' whites. Pat was born on St. Joseph's Day, something she believes was prescient. St. Joseph is the Patron Saint for a Peaceful Death, and her earliest dream was to be a healer.

She worked in intense settings — emergency rooms and shelters — before Hospice. But even in the worst hours, Pat was unafraid, recalling her father's strong example. "I'm a farmer's daughter. I understand the seasons, the circle of life."

"You go where you know you should go. Honor the spirit in your heart and take those paths that lead you to your fulfillment…I feel fortunate that I have been in the right place," Pat says, before moving down the hallway and through an open door.

— *Pat,* BEACON PLACE

Well-meaning caretakers sometimes attempt to redirect the experience of another's illness. Caretaking involves active attention to the patient's expressed needs.

SHE WAS 40 when her hand touched a lump within her breast that led to surgery, chemotherapy, and change. Her baby son was four; her eldest child was 13. Theresa's youngest crept into her bed and asked, "Mom, did I cause your cancer?"

"We call it, The Year of My Cancer," Theresa smiles now.

Four years later, Theresa faced something even harder: her husband's illness and cancer. Unlike Theresa, Bill would not win his own valiant fight.

But oh, Theresa says, with shining eyes, *how he fought!* Through rounds of surgeries, treatments, trials and therapies, Bill battled as his strength ebbed. After several years, his oncologist asked Bill what Theresa could not: Could he find the courage to accept what was?

Theresa whispers his doctor helped Bill "put down that fight," and accept Hospice care.

At the end, nearly 1,000 people lined up to pay their respects to her heroic husband and beloved friend.

It was only later, when Theresa would hear her son weep in the night, that her own grief overwhelmed. The Kids Path counselors had supported her children faithfully. Swallowing a hard lump in her throat, Theresa worried.

Hadn't she used up her year of Hospice support?

No, she was reassured. And Hospice stayed with them, Theresa adds, until she and her young family found their long way through the dark night home.

— *Theresa and family,* HOSPICE CLIENTS

"*Human beings, vegetables, or cosmic dust,*
    we all dance to a mysterious tune, intoned in the distance by an invisible player."
        – Albert Einstein

HER HAIR IS A RIOT OF CURLS and her whole

face curves into a smile. Holly, a social worker, sometimes bakes brownies, or cranks up country music, or does whatever it takes to cajole her way into a patient's trust. Social workers were once called "friendly visitors," Holly explains.

Visits sometimes segue into a life review. Holly "gets out of the way" of the flow of past experiences, loves, and hopes that sometimes rush out from patients. These are the "final gifts," the delicate flotsam of the spirit.

Holly was once in a serious auto accident leaving her paralyzed. Broken and bruised, she discovered what she describes as the "sweet center" of life.

"So often the source of suffering is an emotional thing, a spiritual thing," Holly says. She helps her patients detect that same sweet center in the midst of struggle. The process keeps her "alive, and raw, and grounded."

"I don't have a bag — a blood pressure tool. There's nothing but me…a visitor with a purpose."

— *Holly,* HOME CARE SOCIAL WORK

Hospice staff and volunteers advise family and friends to not avoid the ill but instead to schedule visits or outings. Bringing music, flowers, pictures, posters, or even treats for the patient or their family is also helpful. Allow them to suggest ways you can be of help.

KAREN IS UPBEAT. Her snowy white hair is freshly washed

and styled. Her daughter Kelly jiggles an infant granddaughter as mother and daughter exchange smiles. Identical cornflower blue eyes meet affectionately. A wall is plastered with family photos, cards, and tender notes scribbled in crayon.

Karen's husband, Joe, 81, has visited the Hospice residence nightly for months. Relinquishing her care was hard for him, she observes. "I thought, 'He's so good! But this is too much for him.' It's hard to watch somebody suffer like that."

Karen praises her social worker, nurses, the Hospice staff, and especially her doctor, despite the fact that the cancer is incurable. "The best thing that ever happened to me is coming to Hospice. This is fabulous. I couldn't believe that people could be so nice."

"My body has some problems, but my spirit is fine," Karen insists, glancing through a French door into the garden. She adds, "I would like for everybody to know what we're going through here, and how *good* this place is for people."

Does Hospice now feel a bit like home? The blue eyes intensify. "Yes it does," Karen replies. "It *sure does*."

— *Karen,* 80, BEACON PLACE PATIENT

"The aim of life is to live, and to live means to be aware, joyously, serenely, divinely aware."
— Henry Miller

THE BOOKS Martha can no longer read are shelved; audio books fill the stand beside her chair. Her dimming blue eyes are wise and knowing; her white hair is neatly styled. An oxygen tube feeds her lungs whenever she pauses for a deep breath.

She holds an envelope labeled "Foolishness," filled with stories, clippings, and cartoons supplied by friends. She pulls these out when she and her daughter, who has Parkinson's disease, need a good laugh. Martha especially favors jokes that poke fun at the elderly. She tells three with expert comic timing.

"If you can't laugh at yourself when you're older, you're in trouble," Martha says impishly. "It makes you feel better if you keep a smile on your face."

"You can sit and grouse that your knee is hurting, or you can find something funny in it," Martha points out. Her Hospice nurse, Wendy, sits nearby; their eyes meet affectionately.

Martha sighs that she has enjoyed the glorious day. But her heart is failing, Martha explains. She calmly says she is ready to die.

"She tells me she needs a joke more than she needs pills," Wendy smiles. When Wendy phoned the pharmacy Martha requested jokes. It took three tries to produce someone who could fill that prescription, Martha tells merrily. "But they did!"

— *Martha*, 92, HOME CARE PATIENT

Pets offer comforting, unconditional love to their ill owners.
Offer to walk a patient's dog, or bring pet treats.

LYNN HAD OFTEN OBSERVED pets displaced by illness. It was happening again.

Boris the cat always made the Hospice nurse smile whenever she visited her patient. He reminded her of her own black and white cat named Domino. Boris first played aloof, but soon rushed to greet Lynn on arrival.

Boris landed in solitary confinement after pawing the patient in greeting, accidentally tearing her paper-thin skin. The patient's family banished Boris to a screened porch, far removed. Now Lynn could hardly bear to see the cat's pleading green eyes.

Lynn fretted. *What would happen to Boris?* A month after the patient's death, the family left a message for her: Boris was hers if she wanted. Lynn took Boris home to join her menagerie — dogs Mikki and Sunny, and Domino the cat. All were rescues; one of her dogs walked with the aid of an orthotic.

"Boris would beat up on Domino," Lynn laughs with moist eyes, "but was wonderful with people."

Boris died peacefully last April, surrounded by his big-hearted surrogates.

— *Lynn,* HOME CARE NURSE

"The call of death is a call of love. Death can be sweet if we answer it in the affirmative, if we accept it as one of the great eternal forms of life and transformation."

— *Hermann Hesse*

THE UNMISTAKABLE smell of chicken frying fills the Hospice residence. The doctor studies a patient's record, absorbed. He's a slender, poised man, with eyes the color of chocolate. A staff person offers him a tray of food; Gus gratefully accepts.

Gus loves Thursdays at Hospice. "Somebody said you can tell a lot about a culture by how they are dealing with their most helpless people," he explains. The terminally ill are surely the most helpless, having lost both their economic and physical power.

Gus deeply admires his oncology patients, describing clear, committed relationships with their doctor. "They wish to be taught. They're open, motivated…happy." Scores of patients later, he describes his very first case, adding thoughtfully, "I think I have the best job in the world."

Gus, the physician, has lived other lives: writer, social worker, and ardent hiker, who trekked throughout Britain, India, and Nepal. He once drove a Volkswagen van from Munich to Pakistan. He's also discovered whistling, and enters competitions.

There's no whistling school, Gus smiles. *You simply learn on your own.* "Everyone does it differently."

Gus' pager beeps; he rises to join a patient waiting behind a door. The storm lifts outside; gray clouds part to allow sunlight. As he walks away, a nurse nods at his retreating back, mouthing, "Isn't he amazing?"

— *Gus*, ONCOLOGIST

Children are often exquisitely attuned to problems, intuiting them before they are directly informed. The old notions about "protecting" children by withholding information can lead to even deeper trauma and chaos for a child.

MARION, A NURSE and administrator, works in pediatrics.
Hospice work fitted her sense that truth itself was as powerful as any
medical intervention offered. The approach seemed instinctual, allowing
Marion to offer the gentle truth to any patient who sought it.

Again and again, patients eventually asked: *could they become well?
And if not, could they return home to die?* Even the youngest of Marion's
patients wanted an honest, open friend to turn to at life's edge.

Marion offered what was needed as gently and soothingly as possible.
Once as Marion sat with a patient, a small bird came to rest on the
window sill within view.

"That was the moment the child died," she says softly. Marion felt
deeply comforted as the bird took flight.

The end of life could be a gentle as the rustle of a wing, Marion
thought suddenly; a euphoric release and beautiful transition.

— *Marion,* KIDS PATH

"If we are lucky, well before we die we will have no secrets that cannot be shared, no doors and windows that we are afraid to leave open to the world, and thus no fear of living."

— *Freeman Patterson*

IT IS FRIDAY THE 13TH, but the fact doesn't scare Jack a bit. In fact, his eyes dance while recounting occasions when he's hoisted up his guitar and sung.

Jack sings on request at meetings, bedside vigils, and funerals. He recently sang "Be Not Dismayed" with a lady as she took communion from her bed. When Jack isn't singing, he's writing about the tempering experiences that infuse his voice and songs.

He wrote about an unflappable 90-year-old, whose house burned down. Jack wrote about Mildred, the patient who dug up lilies to give away at the end of her life. The strange holes he had noticed in her garden "weren't dead spaces."

"She saw them as living spaces." Jack noted after Mildred explained.

"When you listen to people's story, it takes time. And I'm always aware God is already in places I haven't dared to go." There is often laughter, song, and great humor punctuating a patient's journey.

A patient once smiled and clasped Jack's hand, whispering, "Religion is for people who are afraid of going to hell. Spirituality is for people who have been there."

— *Jack,* CHAPLAINCY AND
BEREAVEMENT COUNSELING

Gently invite the sick or the grieving to join you in activities, without insisting.
Engagement with things they have always enjoyed is therapeutic and comforting.

MIKE SQUINTS AT THE SKY as he retrieves the paper. The weather, of course, will make a difference in his planning. So will how his friend, Joe, feels today. If both cooperate, Mike, a Hospice volunteer, will pick up Joe, a patient, for their customary afternoon drive.

The two men meet Saturdays, irrespective of the weather. They stay indoors if the weather's poor, but "when it's bright and dry, we pack up Joe's oxygen tank and hit the road." Mike is a professor, writer, and lover of jazz. Joe is a professional musician. Mike jokingly calls Joe "Miss Daisy," a reference to the movie and his friend's "exacting taste."

Like the very best road trips, the end point is unimportant. Their destination's secondary. Sometimes the drive is nostalgic; sometimes musing. They visit former homes, hot spots where Joe once played, or a city park. Sometimes, they simply observe construction sites and signs of progress around town.

But in the car, alone together, the pair resume their journey to wherever the spirit moves them. Only the Duke, Coltrane, and Miles Davis are invited along.

A note sounds, low and sweet, as the pair follow its lead.

— *Mike,* HOME CARE VOLUNTEER

"Nothing that was worthy in the past departs;
    no truth or goodness realized by man ever dies, or can die."
                    — Thomas Carlyle

THE NOONDAY SUN beats down on the new fishermen at a camp created for bereaved children. Ben tensely waits for a fish to bite. Ashley, a slip of a girl, screams, "I catched a fish! I catched a fish!" and wiggles in a joyful dance. A disgusted Ben throws down his pole, announcing he's leaving.

Ashley and newfound friend Nicole walk thoughtfully up the hill to another activity.

Someone asks, "What is Ben carrying?"

"A lot," Nicole whispers.

Ben returns; his mood has lightened. He cheerfully rejoins the group, now beading necklaces. As they bead, Ashley describes her father's illness. Ben listens intently, interjecting he also lost his father.

"Being with friends gets my mind off it," Ben admits. "It makes me feel like I'm not the only one."

Murmurs fill the room. Children discuss lost fathers, brothers, sisters, mothers, grandparents. The counselors ask they share happy memories for the closing ceremonies that night. Ben waves his hand.

"I think of my dad because he took so many pictures of sunsets," Ben says. "Dad said you had to watch the whole thing...He taught me to watch the *whole thing*."

The children nod wordlessly in understanding, and Ben seems cheered, almost changed, by their knowing looks.

— *Kids Path Bereavement Camp*

People who are ill also need to live creatively and meaningfully. Stephen Levine notes that the beginning of healing for both the living and the dying "is the end of life unlived."

DURING ANDREA'S DAY she travels between Stokesdale

and Julian, seeing four or five Hospice clients. She replays events afterwards, extracting information. These insights, Andrea says, "are the best part of the counseling job."

Over time, one of her artistic patients decided to resume painting. They told Andrea, "I'm inspired again. I'm going to finish that painting!"

"We assist with helping people accomplish goals. People think Hospice patients are all comatose. Not true! Some of my patients are driving, taking trips...Once Hospice comes in, we're here to help you live."

Unlike nurses who can offer more immediate support, Andrea explains, counselors cannot. Yet slowly, they can ameliorate the pain. "We can't give you a pill and it help. A nurse wants to know what, where, the duration of the pain, and what hurts it. With counseling, I only get to *'What hurts?'* The next time I may dig a little deeper."

Driving away, Andrea cranks up the music of Kenny G. It speaks of gentle beginnings and movements that build towards finales. The clarinet sounds a graceful note in Andrea's ear resonating with her thought: *Death is not always sad.*

— *Andrea,* BEREAVEMENT COUNSELING

"*The hero is the one who kindles a great light in the world,*
who sets up blazing torches in the dark streets of life for men to see by.
The saint is the man who walks through the dark paths of the world, himself a light."
— *Felix Adler*

IN THE EARLY DAYS, Ann gave countless speeches to

fraternities, sororities, women's groups, doctors, and nurses about the
needs of seriously or terminally ill children.

"It was a mission," she says, raking a hand through shining white,
cropped hair. That mission became Kids Path, one of the nation's largest
pediatric palliative care programs.

"The immense gift I was given when I came here was free rein to
create something that wasn't there before…" White explains. The gift
melded into reality. "Greensboro was always charity-minded, and open
to *'What can I do for my neighbor?'*"

Fellow educators, parents, and the children served became Ann's
teachers. She speaks the names of several children she has counseled
aloud. Her blue eyes moisten.

After 17 years doing this work, Ann is leaving Greensboro, returning
to her Seattle hometown. "The work I set out to do here, I did — and
I only had to do this little piece. Community leaders understand the issues
around grieving better than before Kids Path. They support children and
the grief work."

"Every single one of us grieves," Ann adds pensively. "And we all
need to be better to each other."

— *Ann,* KIDS PATH

It is no cliché to "brighten the corner where you are." The deliberate choice to
create and find beauty, especially in times of suffering, has dynamics of its own.

WHEN SALLY WAS 10 YEARS OLD, her father died. "I remember an aunt putting her arms around me, and her tears dripping down on me. She let me know how she felt, that she was sad. Her tears told me, 'We're all in this moment right now, that we share.'"

Years later, Sally wanted to synthesize her love of gardening with humane work. She heard about horticultural therapy. "I was already volunteering with Hospice and already awestruck by how individual God was. Then I learned that Hospice was building a Kids Path building with a therapeutic garden behind it." She began training in horticultural therapy in Denver. Following training, she was hired.

Sally placed fat pots filled with blooms at the Hospice entryway. Hospice "had this naked doorway. I felt *what we do begins before people even get inside. What we show the world, that's our first chance.*" Young or old, Sally's clients loved the messy joys of gardening.

Sally wheeled patients outside, involving them in work or planning. Volunteers brought truck loads of hostas and lilies, creating new beds. Hospice blossomed; so did Sally. Something mutually therapeutic was happening in with her, the patients, and the soil they tended. The plants needed them as much as they needed the plants.

With one elbow deep in dirt, Sally grins a lopsided grin. "That's where it all started for me," and moves a plant to a better spot.

— *Sally,* HORTICULTURE THERAPY

"Getting a comedic view of your situation gives you spiritual distance. Having a sense of humor saves you."

— *Joseph Campbell*

HE IS A MAN OF STRENGTH. He spent his life in

public service, directing the city's largest human services organization. But a few weeks earlier, he was torn from his old life when he fell in the middle of the night. An MRI revealed a walnut-sized tumor in his brain. Dave's strength ebbed as rapidly as a walnut rolling across a floor.

Dave is spending the remaining days owed to him in the Hospice unit. His family gather as he hovers at the edge of life. Sometimes he is seeing and present. Other times he is unseeing and staring. At times his fist is clutched and sometimes his palm is open. Last week, his son brought his beloved Golden Retriever to his bedside. The dog laid his head on his master's chest, and sighed.

"I don't know who needs one another more right now," Dave's wife observed.

Friends come and go from Dave's room. A favorite nurse turns him because he cannot turn himself.

Peace is creeping into the small space containing his life. When Dave is not napping, there is laughter. He asks when Happy Hour will be. His wife tsks, tsks. "Would you like some chopped fruit?"

"Some chopped Scotch," he grumps, and winks. The humor that hallmarked his life is now gracing his death.

— *Dave,* 85, HOSPICE UNIT PATIENT

Madeleine L'Engle described the death of her son as the vivid experience of
living in a "wild" universe of frightening truths. But she added her creativity
sprang from "seeing everything — even when you want to shut your eyes."

MAURA HAD LOST HER CHILD, Lucy, four years

earlier. When the worst of her own grief's raging tides abated, Maura enrolled in volunteer training for Kids Path, a specialized program for seriously ill or bereaved children. After training, Maura was matched with a 2½ year old toddler named Nicki.

Each week Maura played with Nicki, giving her parents a respite. The pair sometimes sang Winnie the Pooh songs, or more often played with Barbie dolls as Nicki bravely endured chemotherapy and treatments. Maura and the child developed an intimate bond, as Nicki steadily worsened.

A year later, Maura was obliged to leave on a family trip to Norway. Maura reluctantly said good-bye to Nicki, believing their parting was final.

Maura traveled to a remote area of Norway to hike; with her gear she also carried the heaviness of her sorrow for the little girl. While hiking she witnessed a double rainbow, and immediately intuited that Nicki had died.

Maura returned to Oslow, making contact with Nicki's father. He confirmed her intuition about Nicki. Outside, the weather was desolate; Maura searched the skies, but no sun shone and no rainbows appeared. Maura and her husband decided to take a long walk, slogging along beneath Oslow's darkening sky. Avoiding a puddle, Maura stopped short at the sight of a tiny pink shoe at her feet.

Stunned by the sight, Maura stepped forward. Then she turned back, plucking the Barbie™ doll shoe from the street. She clutched it tightly in her palm. For a long time to come, Maura kept the tiny talisman in a black velvet pouch, always tucked inside her pocket.

— *Maura*, KIDS PATH

"Humankind has not woven the web of life. We are but one thread within it. Whatever we do to the web, we do to ourselves. All things are bound together. All things connect."

— Chief Seattle

AT LUNCHTIME, 20 Hospice staffers arrive with Elisabeth Kübler-Ross's book, *Life Lessons,* tucked under their arms. They also bring casseroles or desserts to share. For eight weeks, they discuss the respective chapters of the book. *Life Lessons* covers all the major themes the esteemed doctor gleaned from years of work with the terminally ill.

As the staffers eat, they digest the lessons Elisabeth has lent.

Pam, Hospice's executive director, leads the first sessions. She explains how love, the emissary of life, brings contradictory gifts. "Love delivers everything to your door *unlike itself."* Pages are turned; heads nod.

If love is the sustaining ocean of life, then fear is the treacherous cross-current that we must also tread. At our most fearful, we feel unloved, and withhold love. We sink heavily and more deeply towards the depths we feared most. Fear swamps and blocks; love opens and buoys us.

Every relationship, every experience brings opportunity, Pam says. *Struggle. Anger. Blame. Patience. Grief. Surrender. Forgiveness.*

"The person we need to forgive is ourselves," observes Susan, a social worker. "We would have done things differently if we had seen another way."

Before the eighth and final week, Elisabeth Kübler-Ross dies. The news is announced as the meeting begins. Slowly, thoughtfully, the group open their books and for a moment, there is complete silence.

Then, twenty pairs of eyes focus on the page. *Happiness,* Elisabeth's last chapter, is the final lesson.

— *Life Lessons Discussion Group*

postscript

> "Life, so-called, is a short episode between two great mysteries, which yet are one."
> – Carl Jung

IF THE ORDINARY can become extraordinary, then the reverse is also true. During the months spent interviewing patients, physicians, staff, volunteers, bereaved families and ardent community supporters of Hospice and Palliative Care of Greensboro, I observed repeated acts of selflessness. The participant's selflessness became an amazing portal, opening opportunities for this book which could not have been possible otherwise.

Everyone seemed keenly aware of the legacy of their stories, and shared them despite the telling being difficult. Even the physically frail were fully engaged, participating in long and often physically difficult interviews in preparation for the book. They responded with directness, insight, and joy. Patients, staff, and volunteers consented to photographs without protest, setting aside vanity, revealing their spectacular essences. It was impossible to be in the presence of this without glimpsing the transcendent, great mystery that Jung speaks of.

We make grateful mention of the patients' interviews and photographs contained within. Dave Atwood, Wallace Compton (pictured with Holly Bessey), Joe Hooks (pictured with Mike Gaspeny), Karen Pinter, Martha Smith, Hope Walker (pictured with Sharon Davis), and toddler Anslyn Wright showed unflinching courage. Some of them did not live to see the book to fruition. By the date of publication, several had died.

Their images, stories, and triumphs reveal the smiling dawn that lies beyond sorrow.

– *Cynthia Adams*

acknowledgements

CYNTHIA ADAMS, writer and editor of *The Extraordinary Ordinary*, lives in Greensboro, N.C. where she writes fiction and nonfiction. Her book credits include *The Mysterious Case of Sir Arthur Conan Doyle, Carolina Preserves,* and *Village of Pinehurst.* She has received writing awards from the North Carolina Press Association and the University Continuing Education Association, and was a finalist for the Carolina Novel Award in 2000.

ANITA WILSON AND CHRIS WILSON, creative directors of 29 & Company in Greensboro, N.C., created the cover and design for *The Extraordinary Ordinary*. In addition to publication design, their award-winning design portfolio includes packaging, corporate identity and advertising for regional, national and international clients.

CYANA BRILES, owner of Aesthetic Images of Greensboro was principal photographer for *The Extraordinary Ordinary*. Cyana's work frequently appears in publications and magazines. Her sensitivity to the patients and participants shines through her imagery. Other photography credits include Jane Gibson, whose photograph from the Kids Path children's camp appears on page 50. Jane's photography has also appeared in a publication of The National Hospice and Palliative Care Organization.

THE ESSAYS contained within *The Extraordinary Ordinary* were drawn from over 50 interviews with Hospice staff, volunteers, patients and families, physicians, and community advocates. Their willingness to lend inspiration and ideas to this project were essential. Jane Gibson of the Hospice and Palliative Care of Greensboro staff spent long hours nurturing the project from its beginning. Also Paul Russ and Pamela Barrett lent unflagging support.

A special mention of acknowledgement is made to the staff, volunteers, patients and patient families at Moses Cone Hospital and the Hospice Care Unit.

Grateful appreciation is due Tom McGoldrick of Greensboro for the use of his vintage 1948 Buick appearing on page 48.